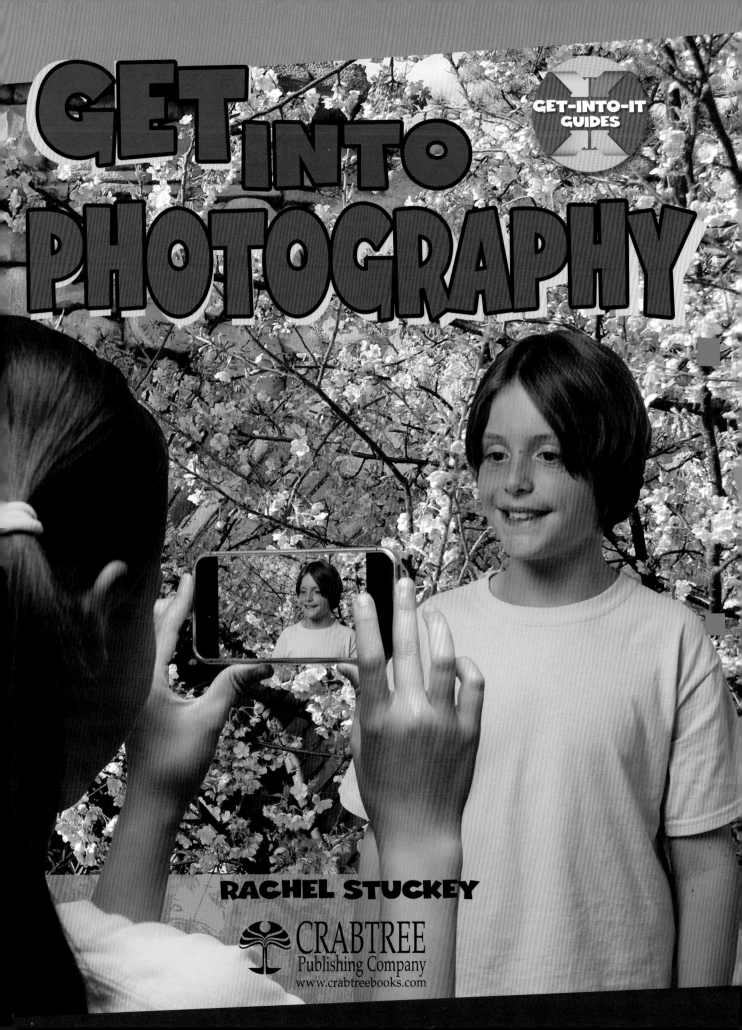

GET INTO PHOTOGRAPHY

GET-INTO-IT GUIDES

RACHEL STUCKEY

CRABTREE
Publishing Company
www.crabtreebooks.com

GET-INTO-IT GUIDES

Author: Rachel Stuckey

Editors
Marcia Abramson, Philip Gebhardt, Janine Deschenes

Photo research: Melissa McClellan

Editorial director: Kathy Middleton

Proofreader: Wendy Scavuzzo

Cover/Interior Design: T.J. Choleva

Production coordinator and
   Prepress technician: Samara Parent

Print coordinator: Katherine Berti

Consultant: John Scully – Youth Empowerment Program and New Media Program Coordinator at The Royal Conservatory

Developed and produced for Crabtree Publishing by BlueApple*Works* Inc.

Photographs

Shutterstock.com: © espies (cover boy); © lanych (cover girl, p. 10 right); © Dmitry Bodyaev (cover top); © Khomulo Anna (cover top left inset); © Phovoir (2cd from top left inset); © PHOTOCREO Michal Bednarek (3rd from top left inset); © (Maxx-Studio (cover bottom left inset); © Sabphoto (cover top right inset); © Denis Kuvaev (TOC); © vlabo (p. 4 middle); © Designua (p. 4 right); © Ivakoleva (photo fact); © Ravennka (blue background, p. 5. 6. 7, 9); © Ekkamai Chaikanta (p. 6 left); © Kletr (p. 6 right); © Scanrail1 (p. 7 top left); © Alexey Rotanov (p. 7 top right); © Renewer (p. 7 bottom left); © Kosoff (p. 7 right middle); © Art65395 (p. 7 right bottom): © cobalt88 (p. 8 top); © PK.pawaris (p. 8 bottom); © taviphoto (p. 9 top); © lkordela (p. 9 middle); © kiyanochka1 (p. 9 bottom); © espies (p. 10 left); © Nicola Gordon (p. 11 left); © I wave (p. 12 top); © Lsa1978 (p. 12 bottom left); © Tanya Sid (p. 12 bottom middle); © Aman Ahmed Khan (p. 12 nottom right); © neelsky (p. 13 left); © Jaromir Chalabala (p. 13 right); © JetKat (p. 14 top); © Ksenia Ragozina (p. 14 bottom)' © oliveromg (p. 15 top left); View Apart (p. 15 top right); © kate_ku (p. 15 left); © Dhoxax (p. 16 top); © ymgerman (p. 16 bottom); © dibrova (p. 17 top, 22 bottom); © llaszlo (p. 17 bottom); © Uber Images (p. 18 top); © Jenny Sturm (p. 18 bottom); © Yuriy Rudyy (p. 19 left); © holbox (p. 19 middle); © gosphotodesign (p. 19 right); © Zurijeta (p. 19 bottom); © goodluz (p. 20); © Patrick Foto (p. 21 top left, 21 top right); © Renewer (p. 21 bottom left); © jaroslava V (p. 22 top); © S.Borisov (p. 23 top left); © Click Images (p. 23 top right); © Manamana (p. 23 middle left); © sp.VVK (p. 23 middle right, 23 bottom left); © mathom (p. 25 top left); © victoriaKh (p. 25 top right); © alisalipa (p. 25 bottom left); © Liljam (p. 25 bottom right); © Patryk Kosmider (p. 26 top); © aabeele (p. 26 bottom); © stock_shot (p. 27 top left); © Artbox (p. 27 top right); © Annette Shaff (p. 27 middle left, 27 bottom); © Ammit Jack (p. 27 middle right); © ZRyzner (p. 28 top); © Viacheslav Nikolaenko (p. 28 middle); © Natursports (p. 28 bottom); © Sergei Bachlakov (p. 29 top left, 29 top right, 29 middle left, 29 middle right); © Robertomas (p. 29 bottom) © UMB-O (p. 32);

Public Domain: Louis Daguerre (p. 5 middle)

© Austen Photogrpahy (p. 11 right, 25 bottom);

© Sam Taylor (back cover, title page, p. 4 left, 5 bottom, 21 middle , 21 bottom right, 24,

Library and Archives Canada Cataloguing in Publication

Stuckey, Rachel, author
      Get into photography / Rachel Stuckey.

(Get-into-it guides)
Includes index.
Issued in print and electronic formats.
ISBN 978-0-7787-2643-2 (hardback).--ISBN 978-0-7787-2654-8 (paperback).--ISBN 978-1-4271-1794-6 (html)

      1. Photography--Juvenile literature. I. Title.

TR149 S78 2016   j770   C2016-903397-X
                                          C2016-903398-8

Library of Congress Cataloging-in-Publication Data

Names: Stuckey, Rachel.
Title: Get into photography / Rachel Stuckey.
Description: St. Catharines, Ontario : Crabtree Publishing Company, [2017] | Series: Get-into-it guides | Audience: Age 8-11. | Audience: Grade 4 to 6. | Includes index.
Identifiers: LCCN 2016026911 (print) | LCCN 2016028628 (ebook) | ISBN 9780778726432 (reinforced library binding : alk. paper) | ISBN 9780778726548 (pbk. : alk. paper) | ISBN 9781427117946 (Electronic HTML)
Subjects: LCSH: Photography--Juvenile literature.
Classification: LCC TR149 .S78 2017 (print) | LCC TR149 (ebook) | DDC 777--dc23
LC record available at https://lccn.loc.gov/2016026911

Crabtree Publishing Company

www.crabtreebooks.com   1-800-387-7650

Printed in Canada/072016/EF20160630

Published in Canada
Crabtree Publishing
616 Welland Ave.
St. Catharines, Ontario
L2M 5V6

Published in the United States
Crabtree Publishing
PMB 59051
350 Fifth Avenue, 59th Floor
New York, New York 10118

Published in the United Kingdom
Crabtree Publishing
Maritime House
Basin Road North, Hove
BN41 1WR

Published in Australia
Crabtree Publishing
3 Charles Street
Coburg North
VIC, 3058

CONTENTS

WHAT IS PHOTOGRAPHY?   4

CAMERAS AND EQUIPMENT   6

PHOTO TECH   8

GET IT IN FOCUS   10

UNDERSTANDING LIGHT   12

COMPOSITION   14

PUTTING IT IN PERSPECTIVE   16

PHOTO EDITING   18

PROJECT 1: PORTRAIT PHOTOGRAPHY   20

PROJECT 2: LANDSCAPE PHOTOGRAPHY   22

PROJECT 3: STILL LIFE PHOTOGRAPHY   24

PROJECT 4: ANIMAL PHOTOGRAPHY   26

PROJECT 5: SPORTS PHOTOGRAPHY   28

LEARNING MORE   30

GLOSSARY   31

INDEX   32

WHAT IS PHOTOGRAPHY?

Photography is the art and science of creating permanent images using light. The word photography comes from Greek words that mean "drawing with light." Photographs are made with devices called cameras. Modern cameras use a lens to focus the light reflected off an object onto a light-sensitive surface or a digital sensor. The image is recorded on light-sensitive material such as **film**, or in an electronic sensor.

HISTORY OF PHOTOGRAPHY

As far back as ancient times, people created images with something called a camera obscura. "Camera" comes from the Latin word for room and "obscura" means "dark." Light passes through a hole in a dark box and inside the box it creates an upside-down image of the scene outside the box.

In the early 1800s, the first photographs were made with a camera obscura and paper covered in **silver compounds**, which reacted to light. But after the paper was exposed to open light, the images would fade away.

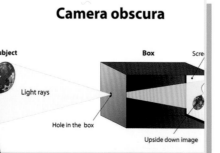

Camera obscura

Subject

Box

Scre...

Light rays

Hole in the box

Upside down image

The image in a camera obscura comes out upside-down because light travels in a straight line. So light rays above the pinhole pass through it and hit the bottom of the back of the box, while rays from below the pinhole end up at the top.

MODERN TIMES

In the 1830s, inventors such as Henry Talbot and Louis Daguerre found ways of using different chemicals to make these images permanent. Daguerre made photographs on silver-treated copper plates called daguerreotypes. Talbot created the first **photo negatives**. The first cameras were very large. They had to be mounted on tripods and covered by black cloths to keep out the light. In the late 1800s, the Kodak Company started making small portable cameras that used plastic film. Color photography became popular in the 1960s. Over the years, cameras became less expensive and accessible to amateur photographers. By the late 1980s, even disposable cameras became widely available.

Earliest known photo showing a living person

HISTORY OF DIGITAL PHOTOGRAPHY

Instead of using film, digital cameras have image sensors that record the light and **digitize** it. Digitized photos are then stored on a memory card.

In 1975, an engineer at Kodak built the first digital camera. That camera weighed eight pounds and took 23 seconds to take a photograph! The first camera that stored images on a computer was sold in stores in 1990. Most present-day digital cameras can also record videos and capture the sound as well.

CAMERAS AND EQUIPMENT

THE DSLR CAMERA

The most common professional camera used today is the DSLR (digital single lens reflex). An image passes through the lens onto a mirror, which reflects the light into a **prism** made up of more mirrors. The prism reflects the image to a **viewfinder**. At the press of the shutter button, the mirror flips out of the way so the light falls on a sensor that captures the image. The photographer can choose to adjust settings manually. There are many interchangeable lenses, including **wide-angle**, **macro**, and **telephoto** lenses.

DSLR cameras usually come with an LCD (liquid crystal display) that gives a live preview of the photo you are composing. Most also have a viewfinder, which is a small window that you look through to see the scene you are photographing. The LCD works well in low light, but can be hard to see in bright light.

Mirrorless cameras such as this Olympus OM-D are lightweight and compact, but more expensive than a typical DSLR.

ANOTHER KIND OF CAMERA

Mirrorless cameras also have an interchangeable lens, but do not use mirrors to capture an image. The image, in the form of light, passes directly onto a sensor, then to an LCD screen for a preview. These cameras are lighter and smaller than DSLR cameras. They were invented in the early twenty-first century. Since they are smaller, easier to carry and use, they are very popular with photographers.

POINT-AND-SHOOT

Point-and-shoot cameras made it possible for everyone to take photos. They are small and light, and have automatic focus and built-in flashes. These fixed-lens cameras have been popular since the 1970s, though many people today have switched to using their smartphone cameras.

Point-and-shoot cameras often have a zoom lens.

SMARTPHONE CAMERAS

Today's smartphone cameras can auto focus, zoom, and have settings for different conditions, but they do have limitations. They are not as powerful as other types of cameras. But they make up for that by being so convenient to use.

CAMERA ACCESSORIES

To protect their lenses, DSLR cameras have lens caps and point-and-shoot cameras retract their lenses. Tripods are three-legged stands that keep cameras steady. A **reflector** is used to bounce light back onto a subject. Digital cameras store images on memory cards, a small square disk that slides into the camera, that allows you to transfer photos from cameras directly to printers and other devices.

Memory cards allow you to take and store thousands of photos. Rolls of film used to take only 24 or 36 photos.

Memory cards

7

PHOTO TECH

SHUTTER SPEED, APERTURE, AND ISO

Shutter speed is the length of time the shutter remains open and the image sensor is exposed to light. A slow shutter speed is used to increase the time of light exposure. This is useful when taking photos at night or in dark places. A fast shutter speed can be used to capture a fast-moving object or to reduce blur caused by camera movement.

The aperture is the opening in the center of the lens that controls how much light is allowed through the lens. It can be adjusted manually or automatically.

The ISO measures the sensitivity to light in the digital image sensors. A high ISO number means the sensors are more sensitive. Low light conditions need a higher ISO.

Aperture

*Aperture is indicated by the f-stop. The smaller the opening, the greater the **depth of field**.*

Shutter speed and aperture must be balanced to get the correct exposure. If one changes, the other will also need to be adjusted.

DEPTH OF FIELD AND FOCUS

An in-focus image is sharp and clear. An out-of-focus image is blurry. The distance between the beginning of the in-focus area and the end of the in-focus area is called the depth of field. Aperture, which is set by f-stops on lenses, directly affects depth of field. As the f-stop number increases, the aperture size decreases. Use a high f-stop number to keep foreground and background in focus, and a low number to make main subject sharp and background blurry.

Portrait mode focuses on the duckling in the center by using a shallow depth of field.

PHOTO MODES

Many cameras offer photo modes such as animal, portrait, still life, sports, close-up, landscape, and auto. Different modes use different shutter speeds, apertures, and ISOs. Taking photos of moving subjects such as animals and athletes requires fast shutter speeds. Portrait mode uses a large aperture to create a shallow depth of field. This makes the subject stand out because it is the only thing in focus.

Macro mode is used for close-up shots of small subjects such as flowers or insects.

Action modes freeze movement with a fast shutter speed.

WHAT IS RESOLUTION?

Resolution is the ability to see fine detail in a digital image. One factor that affects resolution is the number of pixels per inch, or ppi. A high-resolution photo is very sharp—when you increase its size or zoom in, it still looks sharp. A low-resolution image will look fuzzy when you increase its size. On-screen images are usually 72 ppi. Photos that are printed on photo paper must have a resolution of at least 200 ppi.

GET IT IN FOCUS

Focusing a Camera

Photographers can adjust the focus on a DSLR camera by turning the focusing ring on the lens. Most cameras now have autofocus (AF) features. They use a computer and one or more sensors to find the right setting and adjust the focus. Some AF systems have a single sensor, while others have many. To take a photo, press the button halfway down, allow the camera to focus, then continue to press the button all the way down. On a smartphone, you can touch the screen on the point of the image that you want the camera to focus on.

Hold Still

When taking a photo, make sure nothing gets in front of the lens, which often happens with a smartphone. You can also block the flash by mistake. To keep the camera steady, stand with your legs very slightly apart and brace your body. Also, be sure to hold the camera with both hands—if you hold the camera in only one hand, pressing the button to take the photo will cause the camera to shake. Many cameras have image stabilization built into the camera or lens, but it is still important to hold the camera still.

Hold a smartphone at the bottom to keep the lens free of fingers.

Hold a DSLR with one hand under the lens.

Get a Little Help

Tripods were created for the first cameras, but they are still useful today. These three-legged stands hold the camera steady and in a fixed position. Photographers cannot hold a camera steady during long exposures, so tripods are needed when using a slow shutter speed. Typically, you need to steady a camera when using a shutter speed below 1/30th of a second.

To take a photo like this using a DSLR, place the butterfly in the center of the frame. Press the shutter button halfway down and hold it. Then move the camera until the butterfly is where you want it. Finally, press the shutter button all the way down to take the photo. With a smartphone, you would tap on the butterfly on the screen to focus on it.

Project: Building a Tripod for a Smartphone Camera

Use scissors to cut a rectangle shape out of corrugated cardboard. Fold the rectangle in half. Cut a small notch at the edge, about ½ inch (1 cm) deep and about the width of your smartphone. (You want the phone to fit snugly.) Cut the same size notch on the opposite side of the rectangle. Bend the cardboard into a V shape and insert your smartphone into the notches.

A blurry dog against a sharp background means that the pooch didn't stay still for the photo.

Blurry Photos

Several problems can cause unwanted blurring in photos. If everything is blurry, the camera moved while the shutter was open. If the subject is blurry but the background is sharp, it was the subject that moved. If part of the main area of the subject is out of focus and another part is in focus, then the focus was set on the wrong part of the scene. By looking closely at your blurry photos, you will be able to tell what happened and to correct the problem.

UNDERSTANDING LIGHT

Photos depend on both the quantity and the quality of the light. White light is made up of all the colors of the rainbow. When one or two colors of light are blocked, the light can appear blue or red instead of white.

NATURAL LIGHT

Natural light is the light that comes from the Sun. On a sunny, cloudless day, sunlight is direct and harsh. It produces distinct shadows. On an overcast day, sunlight is indirect and it produces softer shadows with blurry edges. The quality of natural light also changes throughout the day. When the sun is high in the sky, the light is bright with a bluish tone. After sunrise and before sunset, the light is warmer or reddish. This is because the sun is lower in the sky and takes a long path through the atmosphere to reach our eyes.

Direct light

Indirect light

Side lighting

Light shines directly, or indirectly, on a subject. Direct light can be in front, to one side, or from the back. Direct light from the side shows the most detail. Indirect lighting is softer, while side lighting is more dramatic.

PLAYING WITH SHADOWS

When the light source is behind the subject of the photo, the subject will be dark. Photos taken at midday have very short shadows. But shadows are longer early and late in the day. Photographers using natural light must be aware of timing and positioning to take advantage of shadows. Shadows can make photos more interesting.

LIGHT IT UP

We use artificial light to add light to a photo. Most cameras have a built-in flash, which gives a quick burst of bright light when the shutter opens. Photographers can attach more powerful flash units to DSLR cameras. Special lights can also change the quality or quantity of light.

A silhouette is a different kind of photo that shows dark images against a lighter background. A good time to shoot silhouettes is as the sun sets.

Taking photos in low light can be challenging, but the results can be amazing.

LOW LIGHT

At night or in dark rooms, photographers change the settings on their cameras. They may use a slow shutter speed to increase the exposure time, open up the aperture to increase the amount of light entering the camera, and increase the ISO (the camera's sensitivity to light). Many point-and-shoot cameras have special automatic settings for low-light conditions.

COMPOSITION

Technical issues such as shutter speed and light levels are very important for taking good photos. But the best camera and perfect lighting don't matter without good **composition**. Composition is the way that the subject of the photo is set up in the frame. What is behind your subject? Have you cut off the head or feet of your subject? Is the scene balanced? Are there interesting lines, patterns, or shadows?

FOCAL POINT

A focal point of a photo attracts and holds the viewer's eye. If there is no focal point, the image will be flat and lifeless, so keep this in mind when you compose a photo.

A focal point can be anywhere in a photograph—not just in the center. Use naturally occurring lines in your composition to draw the eye to the focal point.

THE RULE OF THIRDS

The rule of thirds is a guideline that helps photographers create balanced images. Imagine that the image is divided into nine equal sections using two **horizontal** and two **vertical** lines—like a tic-tac-toe game. The most important parts of the photo should be on one of the lines or at an intersection of two lines. This places the subject of the photo in two thirds of the frame, either vertically or horizontally. Some cameras have grid lines on the LCD screen or in the viewfinder to help the photographer line up the shot, because shots that follow the rule of thirds tend to be visually interesting. You can also improve the rule of thirds composition by cropping the photo in a photo-editing program or app.

Putting a focal point at the intersection of two grid lines will draw the viewer's eye. Horizons typically go on a horizontal line.

COMPOSE THE WHOLE PHOTO

Don't forget to look at the background of your frame. Many photos are ruined because of a distraction off to the side of the main subject. Look for trees coming out of people's heads, overflowing garbage bins in the distance, or people walking into the frame. Sometimes, adjusting your position slightly or waiting a few moments can mean the difference between a good photo and a great photo.

Leaves and trees can be pretty, but not when they distract from a portrait. A simple setting is best.

PUTTING IT IN PERSPECTIVE

Every photo or image has a foreground, a middle ground, and a background. Items in the foreground are closest to the lens, usually in front of the subject. The middle ground is where the main subject is usually located. The background is farthest from the lens, behind the subject. Changing the **focal length** of the lens changes how the objects in the scene are represented. When using a wide-angle lens, items in the background appear smaller than they really are. Items in the foreground appear larger than the items in the background.

WIDEN THE SHOT

A normal or standard lens on a camera sees approximately the same view as a human eye sees. A wide-angle lens sees a wider view, so it takes in more of the scene. When a photographer cannot move farther away from a building or landscape, a wide-angle lens can take in more of the scene. Taking a close-up photo with a wide-angle lens can change the proportions of the subject. Whatever is in the foreground will look much bigger than it does in real life.

A wide-angle lens captured both the city skyline and the trees in the park which repeat the shape of the buildings.

What's the Angle?

When photographers take your class photos, they center the camera to capture everybody's smiling face the same way. But for other subjects, you can take a more interesting photo if you change your position. The viewpoint of a photo depends on the position of the camera. If the camera is below the subject, above the subject, or to the side of the subject, it changes the viewpoint of the photo. Taking the photo from an unusual angle will capture and hold your viewer's attention.

This dramatic shot of skyscrapers and a jet was taken from a very low angle, looking up.

Horizons

The horizon is the line that appears to separate Earth from the sky. Photos of fields, lakes, and ocean beaches all have horizons. The horizon is always straight in real life, so it should also be straight in a photograph. The easiest way to keep the horizon straight is to line it up along the top and bottom of the viewfinder or LCD screen. If you follow the rule of thirds, the horizon will probably be in the lower third or the upper third of the photo. It is normally not in the center.

The farther away things are, the smaller they look in a photo. This is called diminishing perspective of scale, and it gives depth to images.

PHOTO EDITING

When you move image files from a memory card to a computer for storage and editing, you are downloading the photos. When cameras used costly film, people were selective about the photos they took. With a digital camera, you can easily take thousands of photos. But how many photos do you need? After downloading, take time to review your photos. Delete photos that have technical problems such as being out of focus, are too light or dark, or that don't work well visually. Keep the photos with the best composition, and delete duplicates and similar images.

It is fun to see your photos enlarged on the computer. You can check the focus and see small details that you may have missed on the LCD of the camera or your smartphone.

CROPPING

When you trim off the edges of a photo, it is called cropping. Sometimes photos are cropped to fit in smaller spaces. Cropping can also remove distractions and improve focus on the subject of the photo. If you didn't get your composition just right when shooting, photo editing gives you another chance. Crop the photo to make it more dramatic.

You can change the orientation from wide (or landscape) to tall (or portrait) by cropping your image.

Fix It Up

Sometimes a well-composed photo has bad lighting. But you can fix this using photo editing software. Most software will make automatic adjustments when you click on buttons such as "enhance" or "brighten" or "sharpen." These programs let you "fix red-eye" or "retouch." But you can also manually edit a photo by making adjustments to several aspects of the image. You can lower the effect of light exposure, brighten the colors, or increase the contrast between light and dark. You can also rotate a photo if you want to change where the horizon is placed in the image.

PHOTO FACT

Like a camera aperture, our pupils expand in low light to take in more light. A camera flash sends a burst of light so quickly that our pupils cannot adjust. This causes red-eye in photos because the light reflects off the backs of our eyes through our pupils as red light.

Correct color

Increase contrast

Increase brightness

SPECIAL EFFECTS FILTERS

Another way to adjust a digital photo is to apply a special effects filter. Photo editing software and smartphone apps have special filters that change the way the image looks. Some special effects filters change the light level or the way the color looks. Other filters blur the edges of a photo or stretch the image or add a border. Some filters make the photo look like a painting or drawing. These filters can make a photo look more dramatic or funny.

PROJECT 1: PORTRAIT PHOTOGRAPHY

A portrait is a photo that tells you something about a person. Portraits can be posed or candid. Photographers often use a large aperture to reduce the depth of field for portraits. This puts the focus on the subject by blurring the background. Because people blink, fidget, and change their expression, portrait photographers take plenty of shots during a portrait session.

PHOTO FACT

Candid portraits aren't taken in secret. The subject of a candid portrait knows the camera is there, but ignores it. Always ask for your subject's consent before taking candid portraits!

Remember the rule of thirds when setting up the frame on a posed portrait. Try zooming in on the subject. Or change the camera angle or point of view. Ask your subject to look away from the camera or make different facial expressions. Think about the quantity and quality of light. Try using a reflector to reflect light onto your subject and reduce shadows.

In a candid portrait, the subject does not pose. Instead, the subject may be moving or engaged in activity. Candid portraits can be much more interesting than posed portraits. But it is more difficult to control the lighting and composition of candid portraits. A photographer must take many shots to get a few good candid portraits.

SHARING PHOTOS SAFELY

Be very careful when posting photos of you and your friends online. Use your account **privacy settings** to limit access to only people you know. Always ask your friends' permission before you post their photo online. Never post photos that reveal personal information such as your address or school name.

Keep safe by checking with your parents before you upload any photographs.

PROJECT: POSED AND CANDID PORTRAITS

Choose a subject for your portrait. Set up a comfortable place for your subject to sit or stand. Make sure there is enough light. Take several posed portraits, changing the composition, camera angle, and the expression on the subject's face. Then choose a casual setting for your subject and give them a task or an action, such as cooking dinner or reading a book. Take many photographs from different angles and positions. Select the best shots from the first shoot and the second shoot. Which photo do you prefer?

POSED

CANDID

PHOTO TIP

INSTANT BACKDROP

Hang a sheet or tablecloth over a fence for a background. Have your subject stand far enough in front of the background so that they don't cast a shadow in it.

PHOTO TIP

AUTOMATIC WHITE BALANCE

Lighting conditions affect the color of an object, but our eyes and brains adjust so that a white object appears white in any light. Digital cameras, though, need help to do this. That's where automatic white balance comes in. On this setting, the camera automatically corrects the color. Many cameras also have manual settings that range from shade to sun to various types of indoor light.

MAKE YOUR OWN REFLECTOR

Photographers use reflectors to redirect light. They can be any shape or size in white, silver, or gold. Make your own silver reflector by gluing aluminum foil to a piece of foamboard. Put the foil shiny-side-up on the front and leave it white on the back. Experiment with each side when shooting a portrait.

SUN

REDIRECTED LIGHT

PROJECT 2: LANDSCAPE PHOTOGRAPHY

A landscape photograph is a photo that includes features of the land. Landscapes usually show the countryside or wilderness. When photos are taken in the city, they are called cityscapes, and photos taken by the sea are called seascapes. Landscapes are usually wider than they are tall, so they show as much of the scene as possible.

Landscape photographers use a small aperture to increase the depth of field. This allows the lens to focus on the whole scene—both far away from and close to the camera. A wide-angle lens allows the photographer to include distant objects as well as foreground objects. At times when a slow shutter speed below 1/30th of a second is necessary, photographers use a tripod or place the camera on a steady place to avoid shaking the camera during the exposure.

COMPOSING A LANDSCAPE

Landscapes need good natural light, so the sun, clouds, and time of day make a difference. The golden hour, which is the hour after sunrise and the hour before sunset, is often the best time for taking landscape photos. When shooting the landscape, try to remember the rule of thirds when positioning the horizon. Where are the buildings, trees, or mountains in the photo? Where will the eye go?

PANORAMA

*Many cameras, especially smartphone cameras, have a **panorama** setting. Try using this setting for your landscape. Rotate the camera rather than your body. Be sure to hold your hand steady as you move the camera.*

Project: Landscape Through the Day

Choose a landscape that you can visit easily. It can be an urban landscape, a local park, or the view from a nearby hill or from a tall building. Use the widest lens or frame setting possible. On a sunny day, take some photos from the same or close position at three different times during the day. Take a photo on an overcast day. See how the light changes the look of the photos.

SUNRISE

MIDDAY

SUNSET

OVERCAST DAY

DUSK

Photo Tip

Also take a photo at dusk just after sunset. For best results at night, use a tripod. Set a long exposure time—1, 10, or even 30 seconds—and a small aperture. Many point-and-shoot cameras make it easy with a "Night Scenes" mode setting.

PROJECT 3: STILL LIFE PHOTOGRAPHY

Still life photography involves subjects that are Inanimate or do not move. A still life photo may include one object or a group of objects. Flowers and bowls of fruit are popular subjects for still life photography. Still life can be artistic or practical. Food photography is a type of still life photography used in cookbooks, magazines, and advertising.

Still life usually has a backdrop—this keeps the background simple. A backdrop may be white or colored. Photographers use different light sources and reflectors to adjust the lighting and shadows on the subject. Tripods are also good for still life photography. Using a tripod allows photographers to use a slow shutter speed and a smaller aperture without any **motion blur**. The small aperture will need a slower shutter to have the correct exposure. This will mean an increase in the exposure time, but also an increase the depth of field, so that the whole scene will be in focus.

PHOTO TIP

*Still life is one of the most creative types of photography because you are in control. Try different compositions. Change the position of the subject. Change the angle of the camera. Sometimes changing the direction of the light helps. If you can't move the light source, you may need to **reorient** your still life arrangement.*

Move around to capture different views of a still life. You might even find better ways to arrange your display. Using a tripod has its advantages, but holding the camera allows you to be more creative and experiment with angles.

Project: Still Life

Set up a still life subject of your choice. Take photos of the subject five different ways by changing the angle of view, the distance, the background, and the lighting. Take multiple shots each way. Select the best shot from each group of photos so that you have four photos of the same subject.

Photo Tip

For inspiration, check the Internet or look in your local library for books about still life painting by artists such as Édouard Manet, Paul Cézanne, and Vincent van Gogh.

Experiment with taking still life shots of the same subject using different kinds of light, backgrounds, and focuses.

Project: Building a Mini-studio

You can build a still life photo studio to take outside where you can use sunlight. Unfold a cardboard box or use a tri-fold presentation board. Bend the sides backward so that they support the back. Tape paper to the cardboard. Wrapping paper or poster board makes a great backdrop. On rainy or windy days, set up a table near a window with good natural light. Use lamps if you don't have good window light. Use your reflector to reflect soft light and remove shadows.

PROJECT 4: ANIMAL PHOTOGRAPHY

Taking photographs of animals is difficult because even well trained animals don't always follow directions. Animal photography takes a lot of patience and flexibility. Make sure your pet feels comfortable. Instead of bringing your pet to you, go to where your pet likes to be. Get down on the ground to take photos on the animal's level—don't take all the photos from above. It's best to use natural light, either outdoors or near a window. Avoid using a flash because it can frighten the animal and it causes red-eye.

The closer you can get, the better.

PHOTO TIP

Try this trick to catch your pet looking alert and energetic. When you are ready to take the photo, and your pet is comfortable, have a friend call your pet's name or make a squeaky toy squeak. Then snap the photo when your pet reacts to the sound.

WILDLIFE

Taking photos of wildlife is much harder than taking photos of pets. Professional wildlife photographers spend hours and even days in nature, waiting for animals to appear. They sometimes use **camouflage** and long telephoto lenses (left) to get close enough for good shots. Go out in the early morning or in the evening when animals are out looking for food. Scout out locations in advance, so you find good locations to spot animals.

PHOTO TIP

Remember that wildlife is wild. Never approach an animal in the wild—any wild animal will attack to protect themselves or their young. It's important to respect animals and their habitat.

Project: Animal Photography

On a sunny day, pick a well-lit spot where your pet is comfortable, such as a room in your home with a large window or a local park. Turn off the flash on your camera. Use treats and your pet's favorite toys to reward your pet. Take lots of photos from different angles. Remember to get down on the ground. Try to get one of each of the following shots shown below.

EYE LEVEL

CLOSE UP

HIGH ANGLE

ACTION

LOW ANGLE

Photo Tip

Burst mode (or continuous shooting) is a great choice when you're taking photographs of a moving subject. You will have a lot of shots to delete, but you may end up with the perfect shot! It will also help to set your camera to a high ISO so you can use a fast shutter speed to freeze the motion of your pet in your image.

PROJECT 5: SPORTS PHOTOGRAPHY

Sports photography is a type of **photojournalism**—the photos are meant to illustrate a sports story. Sports photography requires patience and experience. Photographers must get to know the sport so that they can react as quickly as the players, and be ready to capture the right moments. They must also know the best places to stand so they don't interfere with the event, but still get good photos.

Good sports photography is very dramatic because it captures people or vehicles in motion. Professional sports photographers use very good cameras with special wide-angle and very long zoom lenses. But you can use similar techniques. For sports photography, use a high ISO so you can use the highest shutter speed to freeze the motion and avoid motion blur.

PANNING

Panning is a great way to capture action in sports, especially races. To pan, photographers move their body so that their lens follows a racer passing by. This creates an image in which the subject is in focus and the background is blurry, giving the effect of motion. Different sports require different shutter speeds for panning. Auto racing uses the fastest shutter—1/500 of a second or less, and sports such as running use a shutter speed of 1/20 of a second or less. Use a low ISO and a small aperture when panning. Panning takes lots of practice. Using a swivel tripod, rather than moving the body, makes it easier and smoother.

USING MOTION BLUR

Another great way to show action is by using a slow shutter speed. Sports photographers make motion blur work for them! A shutter speed of 1/4 or 1/20 of a second captures the blur of the subject's movement, while everything else stays sharp. Remember to keep your camera steady while using a low shutter speed by using a tripod or by bracing it while taking the photo so that the whole image is not blurry.

Super telephoto lenses help professional sports photographers capture distant images clearly. These lenses look gigantic and they are heavy to hold, but using a tripod or a monopod (a one-legged stand) makes it easier to handle them.

PROJECT: A SPORTS STORY

Choose a sports subject such as a game at your school or local park, or a community race. Before the event begins, take some photos of the participants, the spectators, and the starting line, field, or court. During the event, take some photos of the action. Then take some photos at the end of the game or race. Choose several photos that together tell the story of the event.

Tell the story of the event from start to finish.

Backgrounds add to the feeling of being there.

Move around to get different angles.

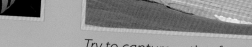

Try to capture action from low angles.

Photograph the emotions after the race, too.

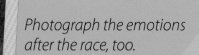

LEARNING MORE

Books

Photo Adventures for Kids: Solving the Mysteries of Taking Great Photos by Anne-Laure Jacquart, Rocky Nook, 2016.

National Geographic Kids Guide to Photography by Nancy Honovich and Annie Griffiths, National Geographic Children's Books, 2015.

The Kids' Guide to Digital Photography: How to Shoot, Save, Play with & Print Your Digital Photos by Jenni Bidner, Sterling Publishing, 2011.

Photography for Kids! A Fun Guide to Digital Photography by Michael Ebert and Sandra Abend, Rocky Nook, 2011.

DK Eyewitness Books: Photography by Alan Buckingham, Dorling Kindersley, 2004.

Websites

NG Kids My Shot
http://kids-myshot.nationalgeographic.com/

The National Geographic Kids website includes a photo sharing site for kids. Young photographers can join the community and upload their own photos.

Kid Photographers Flickr Group for 8-to 12-year-olds
www.flickr.com/groups/48476816@N00/

Little Photographers Flickr Group
www.flickr.com/groups/83295436@N00/

The popular photosharing site Flickr has groups just for young photographers and the adults in their lives.

GLOSSARY

camouflage Something used to hide or disguise the presence of a person

composition The way the things are arranged in a photo

depth of field The zone between the nearest and the farthest parts of a scene that are in focus

digitize To convert information into a series of numbers so that it can be stored in a computer

exposure The amount of light falling on the film or the sensor in a camera

film Flexible plastic strip that is treated with light-sensitive materials such as silver and chemicals

focal length The distance between the optical center of a lens and the film or sensor in a camera

horizontal Being parallel or in line with the horizon, or going from one side to the other

macro lens A lens that allows the camera to focus on objects that are very close

motion blur An effect that makes it seem as though an object has spread out or moved in the photo and left a trail

panorama A photograph that shows a wide view of an area

photo negative An image on film in which the light and dark areas of the scene are reversed, that is, white areas appear black and black areas appear white

photojournalism The activity of using photos to report news and events

prism A glass or plastic object that reflects light through an angle of 90°, so that the image projected through the lens can be seen in the camera viewfinder

privacy settings The controls or filters on social media accounts that determine who gets to see information about you

reflector A surface that redirects light from a source in a different direction toward a scene or a subject

reorient Change the direction

silver compounds Combinations of chemicals which are sensitive to light and contain silver, such as silver chloride and silver nitrate

telephoto lens A lens that magnifies and allows scenes or objects that are far away to be photographed

vertical Being positioned up and down rather than from side to side

viewfinder The window on a camera through which you look to view and compose the scene before taking a photo

wide-angle lens A lens that has a view that is wider than the human eye or the normal lens used with the camera

INDEX

A

angles 17, 27

animal photography 9, 26-27

apertures 8, 9, 13, 19, 20, 22, 23, 24, 28

B

backdrops 21

C

camera obscura 4

camouflage 26

composition 14-15

cropping 15, 18

D

Daguerre, Louis 5

depth of field 8, 9, 20, 22, 24

digital sensors 4

diminishing perspective 17

direct light 12

DSLR (digital single lens reflex) 6, 7, 10, 11, 13

E

editing photos 12-13

F

f-stops 8, 9

flash 10, 13, 19, 26, 27

focal point 14, 15

focus 4, 7, 9, 10-11, 18, 20, 22, 24, 25, 28

G

golden hour 13, 22

H

horizons 15, 17, 19, 22

I

indirect light 12, 13

ISOs 8, 9, 13, 27, 28

K

Kodak 5

L

landscapes 9, 16, 18, 22-23

LCD screen 6, 15, 17

lens 4, 6, 7, 8, 10, 16, 22, 23, 28

light 4, 5, 6, 7, 8, 12-13, 14, 19, 20, 21, 22, 23, 24, 25, 26

low light 6, 8, 13

M

macro photography 6, 9

megapixels 7

memory cards 5, 6, 18

mirrorless cameras 6

motion blur 24, 28

P

panning 28

panoramas 22

perspective 16-17

photojournalism 28

point-and-shoot cameras 7, 13, 23

portraits 9, 15, 18, 20-21

privacy settings 20

R

reflectors 7, 20, 21, 24, 25

resolution 7, 9

rule of thirds 15, 17, 20, 22

S

shadows 12, 13, 14, 20, 24, 25

shutter 6, 8, 11, 13, 24, 28

shutter speed 8, 9, 11, 13, 14, 22, 24, 27, 28

silhouettes 13

smartphone cameras 7, 10, 11, 18, 19, 22

special effects filters 19

sports photography 28-29

still life photography 24-25

T

Talbot, Henry 5

telephoto lenses 6, 28

tripods 5, 7, 11, 22, 23, 24, 28

V

viewfinder 6, 15, 17

W

white balance 21

wide-angle lenses 6, 16, 22, 28